Original title:
Currents in the Dark

Copyright © 2025 Creative Arts Management OÜ
All rights reserved.

Author: Matthew Whitaker
ISBN HARDBACK: 978-1-80587-400-3
ISBN PAPERBACK: 978-1-80587-870-4

Embrace of the Obscured River

In shadows where the fish all wink,
They giggle at the thoughts we'd think.
Beneath the moon's bemused glow,
The river dances, don't you know?

With laughter bubbling in the stream,
They play at being part of a dream.
A turtle wears a silly hat,
While frogs debate—the latest spat.

The rocks all chuckle, mossy and green,
As ducks perform their clumsy scene.
Each splash and quack brings glee to night,
Nature's playhouse, pure delight.

So come and join this merry band,
We'll frolic where the shadows stand.
For in the dark, our hearts will soar,
In the embrace of folklore's lore.

Flowing Through Ink and Silence

A river whispers tales untold,
In bubbling giggles, they unfold.
With paper boats that laugh and float,
In mucky depths, there's joy, not rote.

The midnight fish wear snazzy ties,
While crickets share their witty lies.
A catfish dons a pompous pout,
While laughing stars fling sprinkles out.

Beneath a tree with branches wide,
A party's brewing on the tide.
With nighttime snacks of bugs and glee,
Who knew dark waters could be free?

So let your heart take flight and dance,
In ink-stained waves, we take our chance.
With each soft rippling, laughter flows,
In the silence, humor grows.

The Enigmatic Ebb

They say the moon is full of tricks,
While crabs play cards and swap their picks.
The seaweed sways in unseen glee,
Oh, what a night for sheer esprit!

In shadowed swells, there's humor spun,
As starfish dance, claiming the sun.
The tides are in on every joke,
With laughter wrapped in seafoam cloak.

A dolphin quips, "I'm quite the star,"
While jellyfish float, bizarre bazaar.
The echoes bubble, giggles burst,
In the quiet, mischief's thirst.

So come aboard this merry ride,
On ebbing waves where smiles abide.
In oceans deep, let nonsense reign,
For in the dark, we smile again.

Lurking Beneath the Breeze

In whispers soft, the shadows slide,
Where mice wear capes, pretending to hide.
A hedgehog plays a tiny flute,
While owls hoot out a funny tune.

The wind brings secrets, tales of yore,
As leaves twirl down, wanting more.
A squirrel juggles acorns with flair,
Unseen punters wait, grin in the air.

Lurking low are tricks and pranks,
Beneath the boughs, there are many thanks.
A midnight feast of nuts and dreams,
Where laughter flows like gentle streams.

So tiptoe 'round, but do be wise,
For what's unseen—well, it's the prize.
In every breeze, a mystery hides,
With humor moving where joy abides.

Mysterious Edges of Twilight Waters

At dusk the fish wear party hats,
With bubbles full of laughter, chitchat.
A frog croaks jokes under the moon,
While turtles dance to a watery tune.

The shadows twist in silly shapes,
As eels create their weird landscapes.
A catfish tells the best tall tales,
While water spiders spin funny sails.

Crypts Beneath the Still Surface

What lies below with all that glee?
A ghost crab playing hide and seek, you see!
The clams are gossiping of shady deeds,
While a wise old turtle spills whimsical creeds.

The anchor rests, a party chair,
With barnacles dressed like they just don't care.
A clam shells out its plan to prank,
With starfish giggles echoing the bank.

Whispers from the Depths

Listen close, the laughter flows,
From the bubbles where the plankton goes.
An octopus has a comedy show,
Juggling jellyfish in a silvery glow.

The whispers tease in watery lingo,
A pufferfish poses as a bingo!
Sealife chats with a sassy spark,
As currents wink in the midnight dark.

Nocturnal Ripples in the Abyss

The shadows quiver like jello in fright,
While fish put on their best disco light.
A shrimp's throwing a wacky soirée,
As all the critters come out to play.

The depths keep secrets, but fun's the rule,
With anemones serving snacks in the pool.
Each wave a chuckle, each splash a grin,
In this underwater jest, we all dive in!

Hidden Waters Whisper Their Tales

Beneath the waves where fish may quirk,
A turtle tells a dad joke, lurk!
The eels all giggle, they make a fuss,
While jellyfish float, with no need to rush.

A crab claps hands, gives a cheer,
As a starfish jokes, oh dear, oh dear!
They flash their smiles, with bubbles in air,
In the deep, dark blue, there's giggles to share.

A school of trout starts to prance,
With fins that twist, they take a chance.
Amusement written on scales so bright,
Laughs come alive in the velvety night.

So if you dive where shadows are cast,
You'll find the laughter, a spell that's vast.
Under the moon's soft gleaming glow,
The sea is a stage, putting on a show!

Flowing Stories Beneath Night's Surface

The river gurgles with tales so sly,
As fish compete to win the prize.
What's the jest? Just hold your breath,
The punchline swims and then it's death!

A frog croaks out a riddle bold,
With every leap, new tales unfold.
The dragonflies dance and roll their eyes,
At frogs with jokes, oh what a surprise!

Bubbles rise like words in flight,
As otters play, they hold on tight.
With a splash and a splutter, they giggle and glide,
Crafting stories where wonders abide.

So seek the depths where humor flows,
In every ripple, a chuckle grows.
In the night's embrace, where mischief is sown,
The waters whisper, you're never alone!

Ripples in the Forgotten Flow

In a stream where ducks lose their hats,
Fish throw parties, and dance like brats.
Frogs croak jokes in a quacky tone,
While turtles chill on their slimy throne.

A squirrel slipped on a banana peel,
Laughed by the reeds, it gave a squeal.
The water snickers and bubbles up,
As otters giggle in their own little sup.

Bubbles rise like jokes in the air,
Each one a laughter, floating with flair.
The willow weeps, but it's not with dread,
It's just the tickles from the fishy spread!

So here we roam where the silly dwell,
In the waters where laughter loves to swell.
Join the folly—come take a peek,
At the stream of cheer, it's quite unique!

Whispers Beneath the Waves

Under the surface, gossips flow,
Of fish in tuxedos, stealing the show.
Crabs tell tales with a pinch and a poke,
While eels share secrets with a wink and a joke.

Starfish argue over who's the best star,
While seahorses race in a glorious spar.
An octopus rolls its eyes, oh so sly,
As bubbles erupt in a glittery sigh.

Currents twist like a dance on the floor,
With turtles moonwalking, who could ask for more?
The jellyfish float with artistic flair,
"Who wore it best?" is the question in air!

Count the fins of the fish in debate,
Who can outswim the giggles of fate?
Join the murmur beneath the sea's play,
Where fun makes the night a bright ballet!

Shadows of the Silent Stream

In the shade where whispers flutter by,
A snail tells stories of a grand pie.
Otters tumble with grace and glee,
With shadows dancing from tree to tree.

The owl hoots of a disco ball,
While fireflies wink and heed the call.
A raccoon dons a mask with style,
It scavenges goodies, but stays for a while.

The water chuckles, its surface aglow,
As shadows of giggles begin to flow.
A catfish wearing a tiny bow tie,
Swims past a turtle who gives a sigh.

Join the band of creatures so merry,
Where laughter bubbles, sweet as a cherry.
In the silence, find joy as you stream,
In this shadowland of every wild dream!

Shadows Swimming Beneath

Beneath the moon, the shadows prance,
They wiggle and jiggle in a midnight dance.
Like fish that forgot their proper school,
They flop about, oh isn't it cool?

With a flip and a flop, they dash and dart,
An underwater ballet, a true work of art.
Giggling echoes, does anyone spy?
Those cheeky silhouettes, oh my, oh my!

Lurking Beneath the Luminous

Under the glimmers, they plot with glee,
A cast of characters, all wild and free.
A rogue with a hat and a fishy grin,
They exchange silly secrets, oh where to begin?

A bubble here, a splash there, watch them collide,
In a world full of laugh, there's nowhere to hide.
As the glowsticks flicker, they toss out a line,
Silly jokes float through, so absurdly divine!

Surrendering to the Cloaked Flow

Oh, surrender to whimsy, let laughter erupt,
As shadows conspire, all tied up and sup'd.
Close your eyes tight, don't even peep,
While the playful murmurs stir from their sleep.

With a giggle of bubbles, they burst forth in style,
From murky depths, they emerge with a smile.
They dance and they twirl, oh what a show,
In this jolly jamboree, just let it all flow!

Tales from the Dusk's Length

Gather 'round, dear friends, for tales so spry,
Of trickster shadows that bounce and fly.
At dusk's gentle hour, the games all commence,
In this watery world, there's no need for pretense.

They trade tall tales of the night's silly quests,
Of swimming through laughter, and wearing jest's vests.
With flashes of moonlight, they swim and they sway,
In a comedic ballet that lasts till the day!

Pools of Dim Reflections

In the pool, my face does frown,
That old rubber duck is wearing a crown.
I toss in a penny, make a wish or two,
But the duck just quacks, saying "How about you?"

Wet socks lie strewn all around,
Was that a splash? Oh never mind the sound.
A frog leaps by with a comical plop,
This swim lesson? I should probably stop!

The goldfish gossip with watery grace,
Making fun of me in this silly place.
As I paddle about, the light starts to sway,
Looks like I'm the joke at this fishy ballet.

With a wave and a wink, I bid adieu,
To this pool of chaos that feels like a zoo.
I get out to dry with a laugh and a smile,
Next time I'll just watch from a safe little aisle.

Veiled Waters at Midnight

Veils of shadow drape the night,
I see a mermaid, which feels quite right.
She braids her hair with strands of seaweed,
And warns me of locks that are not for the freed.

In this dark grove, my friends all cower,
While I clutch my snacks, feeling like a tower.
"Oh no! It's a hydra!" one friend screams loud,
But I just laugh, it's just part of the crowd.

With marshmallows toasted, we tell spooky tales,
While the wind starts to dance, and laughter prevails.
What's that? A shadow? Probably just Dave,
He tripped on a log but swears he is brave!

So here we all sit, at the edge of the stream,
Chasing away nightmares, living the dream.
With giggles and snacks, the night feels just right,
Veiled waters won't scare us, not one bit tonight!

Shadows of the Sable Stream

Shadows flicker by, a dance of delight,
Cartwheeling raccoons in the pale moonlight.
I see one trip over a big, clumsy branch,
As it jumps up, I can't help but blanch.

A timid fish peeks from below the rim,
"Why do you humans always look grim?"
With a wink and a grin, I wave my small hand,
This little stream is much funnier than planned.

Slippery stones, what a jumpy affair,
One wrong move and I'm flailing for air.
My friends are all giggling; they can barely stand,
As I plunge headfirst, and they laugh at my hand.

But so what if I splash? The night's full of joy,
With shadows that giggle and gaggles of coy.
We'll dance with the dark, and in laughter we'll beam,
For shadows are silly by this lovely stream.

The Siren's Silent Call

A siren whispers with a voice so soft,
But it's just an owl, who's flying aloft.
Her call's more like 'hey, let's share a snack',
While I'm trying to float, and not fall on my back.

In glittering waters, I see her flirt,
With a passing fish that wears a small shirt.
She waves her fins in a sultry tease,
While I sip my soda, embracing the breeze.

But wait! What's that? It looks like a crab,
In a tiny top hat, oh what a fab fab!
He's dancing on rocks with such rhythm and zest,
Making me chuckle—it's quite the jest!

With each silly splash, I give my best cheer,
As the siren winks, 'Come join us down here!'
So here we all laugh, in this merriment swell,
This underwater party, I must tell it well!

Veiled Ripples at Midnight

In shadows deep, where giggles hide,
A fish in a tux, takes a stately glide.
The moon's a jester, playing sly tricks,
While crabs do the cha-cha, with swaying flicks.

Bubbles burst forth, with laughter and cheer,
As oysters tell tales, far and near.
A seaweed wig floats, with each little wave,
While turtles, in top hats, misbehave.

Jellyfish bounce like marshmallows sweet,
A dance-off begins, oh what a treat!
With rhythm and grace, they twirl and they spin,
Underneath waves, where silliness swims.

A clam cracks a joke, and the fish all guffaw,
As the sea-dogs roll in, with a comedic paw.
With ticklish tides, and humor galore,
The night plays along, wanting more and more.

Echoes of the Unseen Flow

In the depths where shadows wiggle and sway,
A line of little fish prance, come what may.
They wear polka dots, with no care at all,
While sea cucumbers brag, feeling quite tall.

The crabs throw a party, with shells all aglow,
While eels form a conga, all jittery and slow.
With a surge of laughter, the waters rejoice,
As minnows gossip, in their tiny voice.

They race with a snap, to the sound of a tune,
While starfish share secrets, beneath the full moon.
But watch out for shrimp, they're plotting a prank,
With jellybeans scattered, on their green flank.

In this world of giggles, with laughter that flows,
Even the octopus joins in, heaven knows!
With silly hiccups, and bubbles that burst,
In the unseen waters, it's laughter we trust.

Secrets of the Starlit Tide

The tide whispers secrets, with giggles at play,
As seahorses tango, in a bizarre ballet.
They dip and they dive, wearing hats made of sea,
While starfish snicker, 'Is this fancy or free?'

Dancing by night, with a flicker of light,
A clownfish juggles, oh what a sight!
While the jellyfish boogie, with tentacles swish,
Caught in a moonbeam, they grant every wish.

Crabs in the corner are playing charades,
With clever disguises, and comical trades.
Anemones laugh, their colors ablaze,
As the seaweed whispers in rhythmic ballet.

With smirks on their faces, the waters unite,
In the playful depths, where the fun feels just right.
The tide rolls along, with chaos and cheer,
Each bubble and giggle, a reason to steer.

Underneath the Moonlit Surface

Beneath the bright moon, the fish hold a feast,
Inviting the plankton, it's quite the beast.
A clam in a cape serves seaweed hors d'oeuvres,
While dolphins serenade, with funny little curves.

Octopus wearing glasses, looking so bright,
Spins tales of the surface, both strange and light.
With every swirl, the bubbles erupt,
As the eels share jokes, feeling well corrupt.

Stars twinkle above, adding spark to the show,
As a pufferfish puffs, putting on a glow.
With crickets of water singing their tune,
The dance of the currents begins under the moon.

And as laughter bubbles, and shadows do waltz,
The sea creatures join in, forgetting their faults.
In the mystic dark, where giggles can thrive,
The ocean's a circus, where humor's alive!

Echoes of the Midnight Tide

Beneath the moon, the fish all dance,
While mermaids giggle, seeking romance.
Octopus steals a sailor's hat,
As crabs line up for a late-night spat.

Whispers float like bubbles of glee,
As seaweed twirls, wild and free.
A dolphin laughs at a jelly's prank,
While barnacles form a merry rank.

The waves play tricks on sleepy eyes,
With salty tales and winked goodbyes.
A starfish does a clumsy jig,
As boats rock gently, their sails all big.

When night descends, the ocean squeals,
In every wave, a joke that heals.
So come and join this frothy cheer,
In the depths where laughter is near.

Murmurs from the Abyss

In shadows deep, the crabs all bicker,
While fish tell jokes, their tales grow thicker.
A anglerfish grins with its glowing lure,
While sea turtles roll in laughter, for sure.

Giant squids juggle lost treasure troves,
As playful seals play tag with the groves.
Murmurs rise like bubbles to the top,
Where clams debate which one's the best flop.

The darkness hums with comedic schemes,
As fish rehearse their stand-up dreams.
Eels tell stories that leave folks in stitches,
While waves wash ashore all their funny glitches.

With shadows swirling, the night takes flight,
In this watery world, all troubles are light.
So come dive in, splash a bit, be bold,
The abyss holds laughter, a treasure untold.

The Hidden Cascade

Behind the rocks, a stream does giggle,
With whispers of stones that quietly wiggle.
Frogs put on shows in the moonlit pool,
As fireflies blink and twinkle, quite cool.

A raccoon stumbles, tripping on roots,
Chasing his dreams in muddy boots.
Squirrels drop acorns with a loud clatter,
Arguing 'bout why it's not a matter.

In the hidden glade, where silliness reigned,
The trees tell tales, none ever had feigned.
Hares pull pranks that make others flee,
While owls hoot laughter from each leafy tree.

As splashes of joy cascade through the night,
In the dark, the forest feels light.
So jump in a puddle, embrace the spree,
For even the shadows know how to be free.

Nightfall's Silent Rivulet

As night falls down, the waters sing,
With giggles exchanged like a soft, warm spring.
Little fish tease, doing flips and dives,
While snails tell tales of adventurous lives.

A quirky otter decides to skate,
On a pebble path he just can't debate.
Splashes echo as laughter cascades,
While critters in darkness display their charades.

Frogs in tuxedos hop to the beat,
Holding a party, it's quite the feat.
Mice in sneakers race round the bend,
As fireflies beam, lighting up the trend.

So come take a stroll by the shimmering brook,
With smiles aplenty, just take a look.
The mild night air hums softly, a tune,
In the rivulet's hold, there's joy 'neath the moon.

Veils of Dusk and Water

In a pond where frogs wear hats,
A fish swims by, playing with bats.
The lilies twirl in playful prance,
While crickets join a silly dance.

A turtle boasts of winning races,
With a rabbit's smug little faces.
The frog king croaks a merry tune,
Under the watch of a sleepy moon.

Bubbles giggle, pop, and burst,
Each splash of water quenches thirst.
A dragonfly jokes with the breeze,
Tickling leaves among the trees.

As shadows mingle, laughs arise,
Through whispered jokes and silly lies.
The dusk wraps all in laughter bright,
Where mischief thrives until the night.

Ghosts of the Underlying Wave

The seaweed sways like silly ghosts,
Waving to ships with raucous boasts.
Crabs shuffle sideways with a grin,
While fish debate the best way to swim.

Eels are tangled in a daft race,
Trying to win a slippery space.
The octopus plays hide and seek,
With bubble-blowing clams that squeak.

A pirate's hat floats by with flair,
Now worn by a stingray's bold affair.
Laughing waves crash on the shore,
Joking with shouts, always wanting more.

These playful spirits of the tide,
Invite us to join, have fun, and glide.
In watery depths where chuckles play,
Giggles echo as night greets day.

The Moonlit Undercurrent

Under the moon's cheeky wink,
Goldfish plot mischievous links.
A wise old sole shares quirky tales,
Of dancing snails and silly gales.

The sea's humor drifts in the air,
As bubbles float without a care.
Puddles of laughter rise and fall,
Splashing fun at the banquet hall.

Stars participate in shadow games,
Winking at ocean's playful aims.
And all the while the tide will tease,
With swaying rhythms in the breeze.

These frolics hide beneath our eyes,
Mirthful mysteries in disguise.
Just dip your toes, unwind, and play,
In this waterland of whimsy sway.

Dances of Shade and Stream

In the twilight, whispers tiptoe light,
The squirrels giggle in sheer delight.
A stream chuckles over pebble and rock,
Hosting tea parties at their own clock.

The shadows twist with sneaky moves,
While crickets make brilliant grooves.
A raccoon juggles with leaves so green,
In a hilarious act, a comical scene.

Gusts of wind sweep through the trees,
Chasing laughter, playful as breeze.
Fireflies blink in starry jest,
Inviting all to take a rest.

The water twinkles with mirthful pride,
Inviting everyone for a ride.
In this magical realm, take your chance,
Join the joyful woodland dance!

Unseen Forces of the Starlit Stream

The fishes giggle beneath the moon,
Swapping tales like a late-night tune.
With wiggly tails, they dance with glee,
In a flowing giggle, wild and free.

The shadows twirl, a slippery crew,
Playing hide and seek, they sneak past you.
A clam shell laughs, its pearls on display,
Who knew the tide had such tricks to play?

With bubbles bursting in a splashy cheer,
The crabs join in with a clattering beer.
Under the surface, the pranks unfold,
A slippery comedy, a sight to behold.

As stars wink down on the watery stage,
The night chuckles softly, page by page.
So if you wander where the ripples gleam,
Remember the laughter that lights up the stream.

Veil of the Whispering Waters

The brook babbles secrets in sly tones,
While frogs debate their ancient drones.
Each ripple a whisper, a giggling joke,
As turtles chuckle and fish play croak.

Beneath the surface, the eels play pranks,
They wiggle and squirm with their slippery ranks.
A heron's puzzled, with a bemused stare,
What's going on in this watery lair?

The reeds sway gently, like a dance so grand,
They nod to the rhythm of an unseen band.
Crickets play bass, while the minnows sing,
Creating a symphony, oh what a fling!

In the moon's soft glow, there's mischief afoot,
The splashes and ripples are hard to refute.
So if you listen close to the water's chat,
You might just catch the giggles it spat.

Abyssal Echoes of the Night

In the depths where the shadows play,
There's a ruckus that bubbles in a toothy way.
Goblins with gills in silly disguise,
Throwing a party, oh what a surprise!

The lanternfish light up their funky dance,
Inviting the barnacles to join in a trance.
With waves of laughter that tickle the dark,
They sparkle and wink, each one a little spark.

As squids make sketches with inky delight,
The octopuses groove, oh, what a sight!
The clowns of the deep love to jest and tease,
Creating a riptide of playful mischief with ease.

But beware the tickles from the kelp's dark sway,
For sea urchins laugh in a prickly ballet.
So dive if you dare, where the fun is profound,
In a realm where the whispers of whimsy abound.

Kisses from the Hidden Shore

The waves blow kisses to the sandy toes,
While sea shells giggle as the tide overflows.
The sand crabs cackle in a bursty sprint,
Chasing the foam like a harmless hint.

With whispers of foam and winks from the sea,
The tides bring surprises, could it just be me?
A starfish grins, oh, just look at my arm,
As driftwood jokes, "I'm the real charm!"

With laughter echoing where the sea meets land,
The seagulls squawk jokes that are perfectly planned.
A splash and a squawk, as the tide rolls in,
Under the moonlight, let the fun begin!

So if you're near where the surf likes to play,
Join in the laughter, don't just drift away.
For every splash carries a gleeful sound,
On this hidden shore, joy is abound.

Driftwood Dreams in Twilight

In the shimmer of twilight glow,
Driftwood dances, putting on a show.
A seal winks as she flips with glee,
While fish giggle, "Look at me!"

Barnacles wear tiny top hats,
Ballet dancers with wiggly spats.
A starfish by the shore sings loud,
Making waves, feeling quite proud.

The moon chuckles, casting a beam,
While crabs rehearse their comical theme.
Each splash of water, a silly cheer,
As driftwood dreams take flight near here.

Bubbles rise like popcorn's delight,
Who knew sea life could be so bright?
With laughter echoing far and wide,
In twilight's embrace, they all abide.

Depths of the Quiet Swell

In the hush of the ocean's hold,
Whispers of seaweed tales unfold.
Octopus plays with shadows near,
Telling jokes only fish can hear.

Crabs arm-wrestle, lively and spry,
With claws high, they reach for the sky.
A plankton party beneath the waves,
Where bubbles burst like little raves.

A dolphin tricks a curious seal,
"Catch me if you can!" is the deal.
As waves giggle, roll, and swell,
Ocean's secrets, they weave and tell.

In the depths, where the quiet sings,
Life is filled with funny things.
With each swell, laughter flows,
In the ocean where joy overflows.

A Tidal Secret

Beneath the tide, a secret lies,
A treasure chest of fishy sighs.
A crab with glasses reads a book,
While sea turtles take a second look.

Anemones wear polka-dot pants,
As clownfish swim in silly dances.
Starfish share tales of lost socks,
While eels tell jokes that really shock.

A wave rushes in and gives a push,
Making mermaids giggle, all in a hush.
With sea foam tickling every fin,
A tidal secret waits to begin.

As laughter blends with salty air,
All sea creatures forget their care.
In the rhythm of the ocean's play,
A tidal secret brightens the day.

The Obsidian Stream

In the depths of the obsidian stream,
Fish wear shades, living the dream.
With flowy skirts, they swirl and glide,
It's a fashion show, come join the ride.

"Notice my scales!" a trout does boast,
As others giggle, "You look like toast!"
A catfish in a bowtie sways,
While dancing krill steal the gaze.

The stream murmurs with laughter sweet,
As bubbles pop and wiggle their feet.
Even the stones join in the fun,
Under the gaze of the laughing sun.

From the dark, the colors leap,
Every creature has secrets to keep.
In the obsidian stream, life is bright,
With funny stories that turn the night.

Depths of the Unlit Channel

Bubbles rise with giggles and glints,
Fish wear masks, appearing like ninjas.
The catfish tell jokes, oh what fun!
A turtle slides by, claiming he runs.

A glowworm winks, sparking a jest,
Underwater parties are truly the best.
Eels twist and twirl, doing a dance,
While the crabs sport hats, takes a chance.

The darkness has laughter, can you believe?
With snickers and chuckles, it weaves and weaves.
Around every corner, a prank waits to find,
A treasure of giggles, a real goldmine!

So dive into shadows, don't miss the cheer,
Join the silly splashes, let go of your fear.
In the depths, so absurd, it's quite the display,
Even the clams crack up, brightening the day.

Nightfall's Enshrouded Cascade

Upside down fish play cards in the gloom,
While shadows chuckle, brewing up doom.
A waterfall giggles, splashes of joy,
As rocks sing their ballads, crafty and coy.

Boulders wink, adorned with mossy green,
Little frogs croak thoughts that are quite obscene.
The owls, wide-eyed, are sharing a laugh,
Telling tall tales of their fabled path.

The moon's silver light gives quite the flair,
As it dances with ripples, swirling through air.
And whispers of jest float, echoing round,
In this party of darkness, strange vibes abound.

So join in the fun, let your spirits rise,
Let slip the silk veil, unveil the surprise.
Nightfall's mischief wraps all in a cheer,
With giggles and grins, the shadows draw near.

The Veil of Velvet Waters

A sea turtle grins, with a wink of his eye,
He's crafting a joke, oh my, oh my!
With waves as his canvas, he paints with delight,
While dolphins spin tales that take off in flight.

Octopus juggles treasures he finds,
With a wink and a nod, he's truly one of a kind.
Corals join in, waving arms in the swell,
As sea anemone whispers, "I'm doing quite well!"

But beware of the lobster, he's quite full of tricks,
With claws that snap and logical kicks.
He'll tickle your toes till you squeal with surprise,
In these velvet waters, laughter never dies.

So float in the mirth, let the delight engulf,
With bubbles of humor, and wit that won't shelf.
Beneath the smooth surface, joy's swimming about,
In the veil of the waters, have fun and don't pout!

Twilight's Unfathomable Depth

As dusk creeps in, shadows gather near,
A hermit crab wears bling, giving a sneer.
Seahorses waltz, tails curled in a twist,
While plankton perform, they simply can't miss!

In this magical place where oddities thrive,
The clam jokes around, feeling quite alive.
Starfish play games, "Bet you can't catch!"
And cheeky little minnows, oh, how they hatch!

The glow of the water is sparkling with glee,
As shadows flicker a tune, calling to me.
A tune of giggles, a sprinkle of fun,
While turtles do flips, oh, look at them run!

Dive into the depth, let your heart take flight,
Join in the frolic as day turns to night.
In twilight's embrace, where wisdom seems sparse,
Beneath unforgettable waves, joy will amass.

The Hidden Course of the Evening

When shadows stretch like lazy cats,
I sip my tea, admit my chats.
The moon pretends to be a spy,
While owls in glasses wink and fly.

The streetlamps flicker, play a tune,
As squirrels dance beneath the moon.
I laugh as ghostly figures creep,
They're just my friends who skipped their sleep.

The breeze delivers whispers light,
Of mischief masked by starry night.
Cats in capes propose a game,
To chase those shadows without shame.

So here I sit, a curious bloke,
With laughter rising like a smoke.
The evening spins, the oddities twirl,
In this hidden path, I give a whirl.

Echoes of the Unfathomable Tide

In puddles deep, reflections sway,
Mermaids giggle, come what may.
A crab with shades takes a stroll,
While fishies gossip, quite the goal.

Seashells whisper, tales untold,
Of treasure hunts and socks of gold.
The tides have jokes, oh what a ride,
With giggles nestled in the tide.

Starfish wear hats, so very fine,
With jellybeans that taste like wine.
As waves roll in, they scoop a laugh,
Every nibble pulls a silly gaffe.

So come along, the night's a treat,
With echoes dancing on our feet.
In whimsical ways, we slip, we slide,
In this funny play of the ocean's tide.

Streams of Abyssal Secrets

Beneath the rocks, where twinkles hide,
The fish all wink, at least they tried.
A seaweed party, what a scene,
With dancing bubbles, bright and green.

The octopus juggles with eight arms,
While clams and snails share their charms.
A treasure chest filled with old socks,
Brings giggles out from the hidden rocks.

The current chuckles, a mischievous breeze,
With whispers meant to tickle and tease.
Coral reefs wear crowns made of glee,
As the ocean sings its comical spree.

So dive on in, find the delight,
In secrets woven through the night.
The abyss knows humor, odd and spry,
In waves of laughter that gently sigh.

Twilight's Gentle Haunting

The twilight creeps like a playful prank,
With shades of purple, green, and pink.
Ghosts in tutus flap and twirl,
While fireflies light up the world.

The whispers brush past, oh so sly,
As owls hoot jokes that make you cry.
A spooky cat does a dance so slick,
With shadows darting, do their trick.

The moon snickers at the silly sight,
As bats form bands, in fancy flight.
Each gust of wind sings a silly tune,
That tickles your heart, beneath the moon.

So join the fun, take a leap,
On this twilight path, strange and deep.
For in the haunting's silly embrace,
Lies laughter wrapped in the night's grace.

Flow of the Hidden Realm

In shadows where the giggles play,
The moon's a jester, bright and gay.
A fish in a tux begins to dance,
While crabs do the cha-cha with a glance.

Bubbles burst with laughter loud,
As seaweed wiggles, feeling proud.
Octopuses juggle with such grace,
Playing tag in a watery space.

Deep creatures tell their funniest tales,
Of socks that swim and boats with sails.
The whispers of the night carry on,
Until the sun peeks, and giggles are gone.

So let us toast to the merriment,
In depths where silliness is prevalent.
Nighttime brings a cheerful jest,
In the flow, we find our rest.

Echoes of Darkness in the Deep

Echoes bounce off coral walls,
As clowns in fins play slapstick falls.
A turtle yells, "Watch out for my hat!"
While seahorses giggle, imagine that!

Bubbly, wobbly fish parade,
In a silent disco, they're unafraid.
Eels tell puns, with slippery charm,
While jellyfish float in party swarm.

Beneath the waves, the laughter swells,
With every splash, the story tells.
The deep is filled with chuckles and glee,
In a world where shadows dance carefree.

With each dive, the humor thrives,
In mystery's depths, the joy survives.
Let's laugh along with stars that glint,
In a sea of fun, a happy hint.

Shrouded Whispers of the Abyss

In veils of night, whispers arise,
With giggles hidden in disguise.
A squid with glasses reads a book,
While lantern fish take a sneaky look.

The crabs tell jokes in secret codes,
While starfish laugh in funny loads.
A whale sings out a silly tune,
As bubbles dance under the moon.

Underneath where the shadows trick,
A playful joke can come up quick.
Mysteries swirl with a wink and a nudge,
As beings of night refuse to judge.

So join the jesters of the briny deep,
Where every chuckle makes you leap.
In distant realms of the night's embrace,
The shrouded whispers find their place.

Tides of the Secretive Night

Tides tickle waves in the giggling night,
Where fish sport capes, and stars are bright.
A pirate parrot sings a silly song,
As bubbles pop and float along.

Nautical pranks in the moonlit haze,
With dolphins flipping in joyful ways.
The sea's a stage for a nightly play,
With secretive chuckles that never stray.

Down below, the wise old clam,
Cracks a joke like a wise old gram.
Tides of laughter roll and sway,
In this hidden world, where we all play.

So fear not the night, embrace its charms,
As laughter echoes through watery farms.
In secretive tides, let's swim and dart,
For humor thrives in the ocean's heart.

Abyssal Murmurs and Hidden Tides

In the depths where shadows play,
Fish gossip about the light of day.
Octopus dons a silly hat,
While jellyfish dance just like a brat.

Seahorses prance in lacy skirts,
Avoiding all the flailing smirks.
A crab cracks jokes about clams' breath,
While seagulls ponder their own death.

Whales make waves with their silly tunes,
Echoing under the laughing moons.
The seaweed sways in hapless glee,
As the underwater party flows free.

In this realm of giddy aquatic fun,
Where every tide laughs, and no one's done.
Mysteries bubble, tickle, and tease,
In the abyss, we float with the ease.

Uncharted Waters of the Night

In the stillness of the midnight sea,
A dolphin plays hide and seek with me.
Sharks gossip like they own the place,
While mermaids giggle, a finned embrace.

Light beams twinkle, like firefly dots,
Pirate parrots squawking whimsical thoughts.
A treasure chest full of rubber ducks,
Swirling through waves, ridiculous luck!

Glowworms weave their glow with flair,
Riding each wave without a care.
Mysteries lie in the jiggling foam,
A chorus of fish sings: "Welcome home!"

Adventures toss in this watery flight,
As stars wink down on the laughter bright.
Join the circus of uncharted schemes,
Where even the currents are split at the seams.

The Current's Enigmatic Song

Bubbles pop with a fizzy cheer,
As fishes gossip, 'Did you hear?'
An eel in a bowtie, slick and spry,
Floats by, giving a twinkling eye.

Seashells clack in an offbeat beat,
As turtles shuffle their heavyweight feet.
A kraken juggles with style and grace,
Creating a whirlpool, what a wild place!

Tide pools echo a chortled refrain,
As barnacles tease in this splashing game.
A sea cucumber throws a surprise,
Pretending to be a sea-monster in disguise.

The ocean's tune is a vibrant ode,
To the humorous twists on this watery road.
Come take a dip in this joyful song,
Where everything's quirky, and we all belong.

Midnight's Secret Torrent

Under moonlight, a wave winks bright,
As narwhals sing through the sleepy night.
A squirrel fish struts in a flashy coat,
   Sipping seaweed, riding a boat.

Tide ripples spin with silly grace,
As anemones giggle in their place.
The Great Barracuda tells a tall tale,
While seahorses sip a seaweed ale.

Pufferfish puff in marshmallow style,
Blowing bubbles that stretch for a mile.
A clownfish juggles with laughter and cheer,
With a wink that says, "Let's cause a smear!"

In the depths, where silliness lingers,
And laughter tickles with aquatic fingers.
Join the flow, it's a slippery ride,
In midnight's 'current,' we all abide.

Beneath the Surface: A Twilight Tale

Bubbles pop with every laugh,
A fish wearing shoes, what a gaff!
Lights flicker like a disco ball,
While seaweed sings at the underwater hall.

A crab walks sideways, oh so spry,
Telling jokes as he wanders by.
Mermaids chuckle, flipping their hair,
While clams roll their eyes at the wild affair.

Jellyfish float with a wobbly grace,
Dancing like they forgot their place.
Sunken ships hold treasure galore,
But it's just old socks and maybe more!

So if you plunge into this midnight prank,
Just watch out for the fish with a tank!
For in the depths where shadows fade,
The laughter echoes forever unmade.

Echoes of the Invisible Flow

The shadows whisper with a grin,
As goldfish debate who'll swim in sin.
A turtle races at snail's pace,
While squid contort in a blurred chase.

Echoes bounce off the rocky gates,
Where sleepy lobsters discuss their fates.
An octopus juggles with style and flair,
But keeps dropping things—what a pair!

Light glimmers on the seaweed's tease,
As crabs make puns that aim to please.
Fish throw a party, it's quite the rave,
In the depths where the sidelong waves behave.

So if you wander into this glee,
Don't mind the waves that giggle with me.
For under the surface, both jumbled and wise,
A merry madness is where laughter lies.

Soft Ripples in the Abyss

Down in the hush where shadows play,
Goldfish gamble the night away.
A catfish tells tales, grandiose and tall,
While eels twist and shout, giving it their all.

The laughter bubbles, a frothy cheer,
As sea cucumbers sip on their beer.
Peeking from rocks, a shy little shrimp,
Says, 'Join the fun! Come take a dip!'

Lights shimmer in the playful gloom,
As jellybeans float, not just a fume.
With laughs that dance like waves on a shore,
The dark holds secrets and giggles galore.

So let's splash about in this merry plight,
Where fish wear top hats and waltz in delight.
For down below where the stillness shakes,
A joyful ruckus is all that it makes.

The Cryptic Dance of Dusk

When the blue turns to black, a riddle begins,
As shadows take flight, and the fun spins.
An anglerfish grins with a toothy bright,
Offering candy for a spectral bite.

Bats giggle as they swoop low,
While clowns of the sea put on a show.
A pufferfish puffs, trying to blend,
But ends up a balloon at the party's end.

Twirling and frolicking through the gloom,
Where sea turtles can't resist the boom.
Laughter ricochets off coral reef walls,
In this curious dance where mischief calls.

So join the gala, you brave-hearted fool,
Where laughter and mystery hover in pool.
For in this twilight where secrets embark,
The style is funny, and the jests leave a mark.

Flowing Secrets of the Night

The moonlight dances on the pond,
Frogs leap in shoes that are quite beyond.
A catfish sneezes, causing a splash,
While fireflies giggle, in a dazzling flash.

Giggling whispers float above,
As turtles try to impersonate a dove.
The stars twinkle, with a wink and a grin,
While a raccoon attempts a cartwheel spin.

Water lilies wear hats made of leaves,
Fish tell tales, as if they're the thieves.
They gossip about the swans on the shore,
Who think they're so grand, but they're just folklore.

Night throws its cape over the scene,
As shadows strut, like they're part of a routine.
The giggling brook shares secrets so light,
Turning even the dullest hearts into night.

Veiled Shadows of the Winding Stream

Beneath the bridge, where crickets lie low,
An otter slips, causing quite the show.
Mysteries abound, without much care,
As a fish wears glasses, just to compare.

A beaver's building a grand chateau,
With sticks and leaves, putting on a faux.
He invites the ducks for a dinner surprise,
But they quack and waddle, much to his demise.

The frogs rehearse for a splashy play,
Claiming they're stars at the end of the day.
While turtles cheer, with a big wooden sign,
That reads, "Slow and Steady, we're feeling fine!"

Winding around, the stream lets forth,
A whirlpool of giggles, mocking its worth.
The moonbeam shines, with a wink so sly,
While a fish in a top hat waves goodbye.

Mysteries Engulfed by Night

The shadows twist where secrets hide,
As raccoons gather for a late-night ride.
A barn owl hoots, but it's out of tune,
As they groove to the beat of the old raccoon.

The stars join in with a twinkle and spin,
While the night drags out, asking where to begin.
The stories unfold, like a fox in a hat,
While crickets compose a silly chat.

A wise old turtle, slow with a grin,
Claims he knows all, where to even begin.
But as he shares tales, he falls fast asleep,
Leaving all the laughter in a giggling heap.

Mysteries bob on the waves of a dream,
As the dark delivers a comedic scheme.
And when the dawn peeks, with a yawn so bright,
The critters all scatter, keeping secrets tight.

Secrets in the Still Waters

The pond is a stage for a comedy show,
Where fish wear wigs and put on a glow.
A snail can't catch up, it's slow and unsure,
While frogs crack jokes about their big tour.

A heron, dressed in a dapper disguise,
Tries to impress, but he just looks unwise.
With one awkward move, he slips from his post,
And the dragonflies erupt with a boast.

The cattails whisper, telling tall tales,
Of brave little minnows that brave the gales.
But as they recount, they snicker with glee,
At the time they puzzled a snooty old bee.

In still waters, laughter ripples with cheer,
Even plants slouch back, now ready to hear.
As night wraps its arms, in a blanket of glee,
The secrets unfold, oh, so happily!

Secrets Within the Flow

Under moonlight's silly sprout,
Fish in pajamas swim about.
Worms wear hats, a sight so rare,
Dance together, not a care.

Tadpoles gossip, splash and play,
Ribbit jokes, they steal the day.
Bubbles rise with laughter loud,
The pond's a giggling crowd.

Crickets chirp a funky beat,
Jumping frogs admit defeat.
Splashing sounds and wiggles thrive,
This is where the fun's alive.

In the shadows, tales unfold,
A frog in clogs, so brave, so bold.
Secrets splash beneath the wave,
In this world, we laugh and wave.

Night's Lament in the Tides

The ocean sighs a soft complaint,
Starfish dressed as saints, oh great!
Crabs in trousers scuttle fast,
Disco parties made to last.

Seashells whisper, secrets spun,
The moonlight winks, it seems to run.
An octopus wears frilly lace,
In the tides, they find their place.

Barnacles brag on tales of glory,
Every wave spins a funny story.
With each splash, a giggle grows,
In the night, the laughter flows.

A whale tries to juggle fish,
But they all swim away, oh wish!
The ocean laughs beneath the moon,
To such rhythms, all must swoon.

The Obscured Stream's Secrets

In the shadows, shadows hide,
A turtle rides a tiny tide.
With a wink and a silly splat,
He makes everyone fall flat.

Worms in capes, they slide and slide,
Dancing under the water's ride.
Frogs recite their best, best spheels,
While fish wear flashy, sparkly wheels.

The stones gossip, wildly bright,
Playing tricks to start a plight.
Bubbles host a quirk-filled fest,
Where everyone's a laughing guest.

Lurking shadows start to clean,
As a raccoon juggles unseen.
In the stream, mischief flows,
In this place, hilarity grows.

Edges of Night's Gentle Surge

At the edge of a wave's deep hug,
A sleepy cat gives a shrug.
Mice in boats, with cheese for sails,
Plotting their next grand details.

Fireflies wear their twinkling ties,
While the night owl softly sighs.
A raccoon plays the tambourine,
In this night, the spirits gleam.

The breeze whispers funny seams,
Sailing ships made of sweet dreams.
Crabs throw a beach bonanza bash,
While shadows dance, with flair and flash.

As the tides retreat, they cheer,
The night's fun could last all year.
With each wave and giggling spark,
The edges glow with laughter's mark.

Whispers Beneath the Surface

Bubbles rise with giggles low,
Fish play tag, like kids in tow.
A seaweed dance, quite the sight,
Octopuses juggling, oh what a night!

Ticklish waves tease the crabby crew,
Sandcastles tumble, as if they knew.
Starfish applaud with wobbly claps,
As dolphins share their underwater maps!

A clam's big secret, oh what a tale,
Lobsters audition for a sea-bound scale.
In this silly realm where silliness thrives,
Even the sea cucumbers crack their smiles!

So dive right in, join the spree,
In the ocean's laughter, wild and free.
Where the odd and funny meet in splashes,
And all of our worries sink in the hashes!

Shadows in the Flow

In the river where the fish do prance,
Shadows giggle in a watery dance.
Turtles wearing sunglasses glide,
While frogs attempt to take a ride.

With a wink and a splash, a paddle they share,
As otters play tag without a care.
The current hums a cheeky tune,
While snails are grooving beneath the moon!

A waterfall's laugh echoes so bright,
Where tiny fish throw a mock fish-fight.
With every ripple, a new prank unfolds,
In this wet world where silliness holds.

So come, take a dip, let laughter flow,
In the ripples of light, see the silly show.
Underneath the branches, the fun won't cease,
Join in the frolic, find your peace!

Beneath the Starlit Veil

Crickets chirp in a comical tune,
While raccoons plan a midnight picnic soon.
Beneath the stars with a wink and a sigh,
Glowworms giggle as they drift by.

A rabbit dons glasses, reading a book,
While fireflies gather for a cute look.
The owl hoots jokes in the moon's embrace,
As a fox does a jig, with unsteady grace!

The night plants whispers, a playful plot,
Each shadow should know, it's all quite a lot.
Squirrels in hats, debate what is best,
While hedgehogs take charge, their quirks manifest!

So gather the laughter beneath the sky,
With creatures that romp, gleefully shy.
In the magic of night, let humor light spark,
For all of life dances, beneath the dark!

Secrets of the Twilight Stream

In twilight's whispers, mischief brews,
Insects hold parties, sipping on dew.
The fish tell tales of the great worm race,
While frogs compete in a funny face chase!

Eels with wigs swim in style,
Giggling as they twist and twist for a while.
What secrets they hide, all drenched in glee,
As the creek shares smiles, bubbling free!

The current teases with a playful nudge,
As beavers enact their lumbering grudge.
Each stone holds a tale, each wave a laugh,
In a world so absurd, it's the best kind of craft!

So splash in the night, let humor rise,
In the soft twilight where laughter lies.
Secrets and smiles, in this stream they gleam,
Join in the fun, it's a whimsical dream!

Mystic Streams of Enigmatic Shadows

In the night where giggles ride,
Mysterious boats of thought collide.
They paddle past with silly glee,
Whispers echo, 'Come, dance with me!'

Bubbles rise from jokes set free,
Like fishy puns in jubilee.
The shadows swirl, a playful league,
Tickling the moon with every intrigue.

Waves of laughter fill the air,
Witty banter, a fishy affair.
The trickster streams play hide and seek,
While shadows blush, feeling unique.

In the mystic waters where we float,
Every shadow seems to gloat.
For in this game of light and jest,
Laughter echoes—it's simply the best.

Undercurrents of Haunting Silence

A stillness shrouded in funny lore,
Where ghosts tell jokes and spirits snore.
They float about, a comical sight,
Whispering punchlines in the night.

With every creak and moan they share,
Tales of socks lost, tales of hair.
The shadows quiver with silent laughs,
As echoes bounce off old photographs.

In corners dark where shadows bloom,
A ticklish breeze rocks each empty room.
What haunts are simply jokes untold,
Spooking mortals, if truth be bold.

So raise a glass to those who creep,
In cozy nooks, and softly peep.
For in the silence, laughter lurks,
With every shadow, a joke that perks.

Beneath the Gaze of the Moon

Under the moon where mischief spins,
The night time crew begins their wins.
With shadows dancing, quick and spry,
Jokes twinkle bright, like stars in the sky.

Each chuckle forms a spectral wave,
As playful spirits start to misbehave.
They hide behind trees, whispering rhymes,
Making up laughs from old, silly crimes.

With a wink and nod, they challenge fate,
Spooking the brave who dare tempt their fate.
But really, it's just a feathered prank,
And laughter flows like a bubbling tank.

So fear not, oh wanderers of the night,
For under the moon, all hearts feel light.
With every giggle that pierces the gloom,
In shadows, we find humor to bloom.

Shadows Awaiting the Undercurrents

In the twilight where shadows wait,
Lurking around for a joking fate.
They scheme and plot with silly flair,
Trying hard to catch us unaware.

With every rustle, a punchline flies,
Crooked thoughts behind mischievous eyes.
The whispers tickle, a gentle tease,
Shadows chuckle as they aim to please.

Underneath the cover of night,
Laughter dances—what a delight!
The air is thick with fun and dread,
As shadows play tricks, but none feel led.

So come and join, don't hesitate,
In the darkness, it's never too late.
With shadows waiting, adrift in glee,
We'll find the humor, just you and me.

Mysteries Beneath the Flow

In the depths where shadows creep,
Fish debate just how to leap.
A turtle dons a top hat fine,
While anchovies sip on their brine.

Octopus plays poker, no bluff,
Jellyfish dance, though they're quite tough.
The seaweed laughs, it's quite a sight,
As crabs do the cha-cha through the night.

Bubbles giggle in a spree,
While clams are having tea for three.
The seahorses spin tales so grand,
In the deep where no one can stand.

What secrets lurk, you might just find,
In the depths where fish are oddly kind.
A party's brewing under wraps,
With laughter echoing from their naps.

Lightless Currents of Memory

Underwater snacks, oh what a thrill,
Starfish toast with seaweed swill.
Forgotten pearls roll in delight,
While snails race on through the night.

Mermaids chuckle, tails in a twist,
Searching for shells on their ocean list.
Whales sing tunes of old-time jams,
While plankton giggles with tiny clams.

Nostalgic waves bring a strange sensation,
As squid create a dance sensation.
With each swirl, memories blend,
Of shrimp parties that never end.

Coral reefs hold tales so funny,
Of fish who think they're made of honey.
As tides pull and push with a wink,
It's a wild ride—now don't you think?

The Nocturnal Waterscape

In the night, all creatures prance,
The striped bass leads a silly dance.
With phosphorescent glow so bright,
They twirl around in sheer delight.

An anemone tells jokes so keen,
While dolphins laugh—a funny scene.
The algae brings a funky beat,
As bubble trails make it all sweet.

Sea cucumbers roll, just out of sight,
Diving deep for a snack at night.
The conch shells cheer, oh what a thrill,
As chaos unfolds with a big fish grill.

Hooked on laughter, the ocean sways,
Beneath the stars, they share their ways.
In this watery world, joy takes flight,
As creatures bask in the moon's soft light.

Sable Hues of Liquid Night

In sable shades, the fish parade,
With sparkly shoes, their plans well laid.
They prance around the underwater rocks,
Finding treasures in unusual flocks.

Crabs crack jokes that make waves laugh,
While otters sketch their next big gaffe.
In kelp that's dressed with moonlight sheen,
A crazy party unfolds—what a scene!

Starry-eyed critters share their dreams,
Amid the shadows and silvery beams.
Napping jellyfish dream of cheese,
As the ocean giggles in the night breeze.

Eels weave tales that twist and curl,
While fish wear glasses made of pearl.
In this canvas of ebony delight,
Sable hues bring laughter to the night.

The Silent Flow of the Unknown

In shadows where giggles drift,
The unknown sings, a funny gift.
Wash away worries, loose your frown,
As laughter flows through this town.

Sneaky whispers, a mischievous breeze,
Causing chaos with uncanny ease.
Jokes on the fish that swim by fast,
Oh, what a joke, they won't last!

Riddles woven in the night air,
Who'd have thought they'd find a bear?
Balancing acts, a duck on a stool,
In this realm, we're nobody's fool!

Mysterious pranks, uncalled for glee,
At the edge of the world, there's a flea.
It jumps to the left, it sidesteps the right,
Who knew the dark could bring such light?

Echoes of Twilight Trenches

Ghostly giggles in shadows play,
As echoes drift and then sway.
A frog in a hat croaks old tunes,
Dancing with fireflies and raccoon goons.

In the trenches where we all hide,
Whispers of jokes on a joyride.
A comet made of jellybeans,
Zooms past the stars, it's quite a scene!

Laughter rolls in waves of delight,
Tickling the tune of the silent night.
A marshmallow cat in a crooked tree,
Winks at the moon as it sips its tea.

Found treasures beneath the murks,
Like a sponge that wears silly perks.
Each turn reveals a chuckle or two,
Mysteries wrapped in giggles anew.

Unseen Drifts of the Midnight Stream

Mirth rides the wind like a secret song,
Where shadows laugh, we all belong.
A boat made of cookies drifts away,
Who wants to join this silly ballet?

Under moonlight's watchful eye,
Glimmers of mischief zoom and fly.
A fish wearing glasses reads the news,
While squirrels exchange their playful clues.

Stars snicker at their twinkling fate,
As a hedgehog hosts a lively debate.
The punchline hits, the night shifts cheer,
Here, every laugh is sweet and clear.

In unseen drifts, the joy just flows,
A symphony of chuckles, everyone knows.
From depths unknown, hilarity gleams,
Beneath the surface, we swim in dreams.

The Dance of the Hidden Waters

Ripples of whimsy in pockets unseen,
Where shadows dance and the air is keen.
Marshmallow rivers twist and twirl,
In the glow of the moon, just give it a whirl!

Wiggly worms wear their finest clothes,
As they scurry with glitter, each one knows.
A parade of turtles, so slow, so spry,
With a grand balloon ready to fly!

Whispers and chuckles, a party below,
As fish tell tales of the times they know.
Dancing shadows with glee in the stream,
What's hidden in laughter can't help but beam.

Under the glow of stars so bright,
Mischief brews under the cover of night.
And as waves swim in joyful trance,
Join the water's silly dance!

www.ingramcontent.com/pod-product-compliance
Lightning Source LLC
Chambersburg PA
CBHW060139230426
43661CB00003B/487